D0256718

OUR PLACES OF WORSHIP

Christianity

Honor Head

WAYLAND

First published in 2009
by Wayland

Copyright © Wayland 2009

Wayland
338 Euston Road
London NW1 3BH

Wayland Australia
Level 17/207 Kent Street
Sydney NSW 2000

Commissioning editor: Jennifer Sanderson
Editor: Jean Coppendale
Designer: Alix Wood
Consultant: Reverend Naomi Nixon MA (theological
    studies), Bphil (Biblical studies). She is a
    Priest in the Church of England and also
    works in Further Education

British Library Cataloguing in Publication Data
Head, Honor.
    Christianity. – (Our places of worship)
    1. Church buildings–Juvenile literature.
    2. Public worship–Christianity–Juvenile literature.
    3. Christianity–Juvenile literature.
    I. Title II. Series
    264-dc22

ISBN: 978 0 7502 4926 3

Printed in China

Wayland is a division of Hachette Children's Books,
an Hachette UK company.
www.hachette.co.uk

This book can be used in conjunction with the
interactive CD-Rom, *Our Places of Worship*. To do
this, look for ⊙ and the file path. For example,
material on churches can be found on
⊙Christianity/Churches. From the main menu
of the whiteboard, click on 'Christianity',
then 'Churches' and then 'Outside a Church'
or 'Inside a Church'.

To see a sample from the CD-Rom, log on to
www.waylandbooks.co.uk.

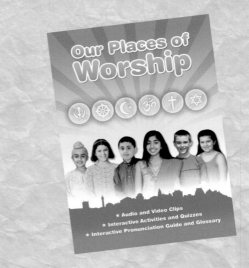

Our Places of Worship
Single user licence: ISBN 978 0 7502 5303 1
School library service licence: ISBN 978 0 7502 5532 5
Site user licence ISBN 978 0 7502 5533 2

Contents

Words appearing in
bold, like this, can be
found in the glossary
on page 30.

What is a church?

A church is a place where Christians go to worship God. There are different types of church buildings, from large, ornate cathedrals to small, simple chapels. There are also many different groups that make up the religion of Christianity. These groups are called denominations and they include Anglicans, Roman Catholics, Orthodox Christians, Methodists and Baptists. Each denomination has its own special beliefs and ways of worshipping God.

▼ This is an old Anglican church with a bell tower. The bell is rung before each service begins. The church also has a churchyard where people are buried.

bell tower

churchyard

⊙ Christianity/Churches

Local churches

Most people visit small, local churches. These can be modern or old. A parish church is much smaller than a cathedral and is usually visited by the local community: people who live nearby. Chapels are small churches and can be found in cities, towns and villages. Hospitals, universities and prisons often have a chapel.

▲ Modern churches look very different from the old churches. This parish church in Surrey, England, does not have a bell tower or a churchyard.

WHAT DO YOU THINK?

Why do you think churches are different sizes?

Why do you think it is important to have a special building to visit for worship?

▲ This chapel was built in 1866. The local people come here for all church services and special occasions, such as weddings.

Welcome to the church

As well as a place to worship, a church is also where Christians go to meet friends, to celebrate special festivals and to visit in times of sadness. Some churches are open all day, so people can go there at any time for private prayer or just to sit and think. Many churches also have social events and Sunday Schools where children go to learn about Christianity, the **Bible,** and to have fun. When people go to church for a service, it is usually led by a minister, who may also be called a vicar or priest.

▼ These children are praying at Sunday School. They will also learn about the Bible and the life of **Jesus**.

The front of the church

Worshippers sit on long, wooden seats called pews, facing the front of the church. At the front, there is usually an altar, a pulpit and a lectern. The pulpit is where the priest stands to give his or her sermon. The lectern is a reading stand that holds a copy of the Bible.

▼ The **congregation** sits facing the altar during the service. The **choir** often sits at the front of the church in special choir stalls, or seats.

The altar

For some Christians, the altar is the most important and the holiest place in the church. It is the table where bread and wine are prepared for **Communion**. In most churches there is a cross and flowers on or near the altar. Above the altar there is often a beautiful **stained-glass window**, showing a colourful scene from the Bible.

pews   lectern   altar   stained-glass window   pulpit

⊙ Christianity/Churches/Inside a Church

The font

The font is a stand with a round bowl containing water that is blessed by the priest. The font and water are used for baptism or Christening services, which is when someone is made a member of the church (see pages 22-23). The font is often near the door of the church as a sign that baptism is a person's first step into the church.

Inside a church

Methodist and Baptist churches are often very plain inside. The churches of other denominations usually have a lot of colourful stained-glass windows, paintings, statues and ornaments inside. Many Orthodox churches are decorated with gold, have marble pillars, and paintings on the ceiling.

▲ Many old fonts are made of carved white stone.

▼ In this Methodist church there are simple wooden chairs to sit on and the walls are almost bare.

▲ This Orthodox church has lots of rich, gold decoration on the walls and huge lights hanging from the ceiling.

Candles and light

Many Christian churches, such as Orthodox churches, have candles and lights that hang from the ceiling. Other churches have lights placed around the church or near the altar. Some churches may have just a single light or candle. These are to help Christians remember the light and goodness that Jesus brought into the world. Jesus is often called 'the Light of the World'. Candles are also a symbol of hope.

STAINED-GLASS WINDOWS

Some churches have windows made of brightly coloured stained-glass. These windows often show a saint or a scene from the Bible. Some churches will have many stained-glass windows that tell a complete story from the Bible, just like the pictures in a book.

A Christian service

Most Christians go to a church service on Sunday mornings when they can all meet together. Worshippers who attend the service are called the congregation. They stand to sing hymns and kneel to pray. There is usually a Bible reading and the minister gives a talk, or sermon. This is often based on the reading and Jesus' teaching, and helps people to understand more about how this affects their lives.

▼ As part of the Anglican service, a member of the congregation may give a reading from the Bible.

Prayers

In Anglican churches, some prayers are said from a special book called Common Worship. The vicar may also pray about issues that concern Christians everywhere, such as a war or a famine. The vicar, or a member of the congregation, may say a prayer asking God to help particular people who are suffering nearby and far away. When Christians pray they usually kneel, put their hands together and close their eyes. This is to show respect to God and to focus their thoughts on Him.

Holy Communion

Holy Communion is a special part of a Christian service. To some, such as Roman Catholics, it is a very important part of the service. It is also called the Eucharist. In Anglican churches, older children and adults kneel in front of the vicar at a rail in front of the altar. They are given a small wafer or piece of bread to eat and a sip of wine. This is to remind them of Jesus and the Last Supper.

THE LAST SUPPER

Holy Communion is when Christians remember the Last Supper that Jesus ate with his 12 **disciples** before he was captured and killed on the cross. During the Last Supper, Jesus gave his disciples a piece of bread and a sip of wine as a symbol of his body and blood. He told his disciples that they should eat the bread and drink the wine to remember him.

◀ The priest blesses the wafers and wine before giving them to the congregation during Holy Communion.

⊙ Christianity/Signs, Symbols and Religious Objects/Roman Catholic Church

Incense

At the beginning of a Roman Catholic or Orthodox service, the priest walks into the church as part of a procession. The priest may swing a container of **incense** from side to side, which fills the church with sweet-smelling smoke. This is to remind the congregation of the sweetness of their prayers as they rise to **Heaven**.

▼ An Orthodox priest swings a decorative incense-burner as he walks through the church.

▲ The congregation in an Anglican church sits to listen as the priest speaks.

Standing and sitting

An Anglican church service usually lasts about an hour and the worshippers stay in the church. Some Greek and Russian Orthodox services can last up to three hours and, during this time, people can come in and out of the church. In most churches, people stand to sing and sit or kneel to pray.

WHAT DO YOU THINK?

Discuss the good things about having a short church service and a longer service. Which do you think is better for everyone? Why?

Jesus Christ

Christians believe that Jesus is the Son of God who was born in Bethlehem about 2,000 years ago. They believe that Jesus was sent by God to save the world from evil and to teach people how to live in the right way. Jesus travelled among the people, teaching them to love God and to love each other. Some people called Jesus the Messiah, which means 'the one chosen by God'.

▼ Many stained-glass windows show Jesus teaching the Word of God to his followers.

Healing the sick

Christians believe that Jesus performed **miracles** such as healing people who were sick or unable to walk, and even bringing people back to life who had died. These miracles show that Jesus wanted to help people and to stop suffering and pain.

Teaching through stories

Jesus told stories called **parables**. These stories taught people to be kind and to help others. They explained how people could lead good lives by not being greedy but by caring for those in need and respecting one another.

▲ Healing the blind was one of the many miracles Jesus performed.

THE VIRGIN MARY

Some Christian denominations, such as Roman Catholics, pray to the Virgin Mary, the mother of Jesus. They have statues and paintings of Mary and the baby Jesus in their church. They also have special festivals when they remember and praise her.

◀ Many churches have a statue of the Virgin Mary.

The Bible

The Bible is the Christians' holy book. It has two main parts, the Old Testament and the New Testament. The Old Testament was written many years before Jesus was born and includes the history and laws of the **Jews**. The New Testament is about the life and teachings of Jesus. It tells Christians how much Jesus did for them and how much he loves them. The Bible is usually kept in the church on a lectern.

Bible

lectern

◀ Some lecterns are in the shape of a pelican or an eagle to show that the Word of God is being carried into the world.

Reading the Bible

Christians can read the Bible at any time, wherever they are. People also study the Bible in small groups to help them to understand what God is trying to teach them. For many Christians, reading the Bible helps them to understand the world and their daily lives.

At home

Many Christians have their own Bible at home. Children often have Bibles with pictures, and some adults have Bibles with notes to help them think about the meaning of what they read. Some people may read the Bible by themselves and think about the meaning of the words. Others may read it for comfort if they are feeling sad or lonely, or if they are ill and in pain.

▶ This young Christian is reading his Bible to learn more about how God wants him to live.

WHAT DO YOU THINK?

Why do you think reading the Bible might help someone if they are feeling sad or lonely?

Signs and symbols

Symbols and religious objects remind worshippers of God and what they believe.

The cross

The main Christian symbol is the cross, which reminds Christians of how Jesus died. When Jesus was alive, he said that he was sent by God, who was more powerful and more important than any living person. The religious leaders of the time did not like him saying this. They arrested Jesus and put him on trial. Later, Jesus was **crucified** on the cross. Christians believe that Jesus died to save all the people of the world.

▶ In Anglican churches, the cross is often empty to show that Jesus came back to life after death.

⊙ Christianity/Signs, Symbols and Religious Objects/Anglican Church

The crucifix

In some churches, such as Catholic churches, there is usually a figure of Jesus on the cross. This is called a crucifix. Many Christians wear a small cross, or crucifix, on a chain around their neck as a reminder of how Jesus suffered to help the world.

▶ This crucifix has the letters INRI above the body of Christ. These are the letters in **Latin** for 'Jesus Christ, King of the Jews'.

THE ROSARY

A rosary is a special string of beads. It is mainly used by Roman Catholics and Orthodox Christians to help them to focus on their prayers. The worshippers touch each bead while saying prayers and thinking about Jesus' life and death.

◀ People can use a rosary in church during a service, at home or wherever they wish to pray.

The saints

Saints are people who have lived a very holy life. Many suffered and died for their love and belief in God. Roman Catholics believe that the saints are their friends in Heaven and pray to particular saints for certain things. For example, they pray to Saint Christopher to keep them safe when they are travelling. There are often pictures or statues of the saints inside Roman Catholic churches.

▼ Saints are often shown in stained-glass windows in churches. People can only become saints after they have died.

S. WENCESLAUS.   S. WOLFGANG.   ✦ S. JOANNA. ✦

Lighting candles

Candles play an important part in both Catholic and Orthodox churches. Before saying prayers, many worshippers often light a small candle as a sign of love and respect. In a Catholic church, worshippers may light a candle in front of a saint's image before they pray to them.

▼ In an Anglican church, people often light a candle to show that Jesus brought light to the world.

SIGN OF THE FISH

Many of Jesus' disciples and first followers were fishermen. They had to keep their beliefs a secret so they used the sign of a fish to recognise each other.

▲ A fish drawn on the wall showed that this was a Christian house.

⊙ Christianity/Signs, Symbols and Religious Objects/Roman Catholic Church *and* Anglican Church

Joining the church

Christians have special church services when they become part of the church. In the Anglican church, this usually happens when the person is still a baby. The service is called baptism or Christening. The priest, the baby and the baby's family gather around the font (see page 8). The priest uses holy water from the font to make the sign of the cross on the baby's forehead and says a special blessing.

▶ A baby being Christened will often wear a white Christening gown.

Adult baptism

Some denominations, such as the Baptists, believe that people should be baptised when they are older and can decide for themselves whether they want to join the church or not. In the Baptist church, baptism is done by total immersion. This means the person's body and head are lowered under the water for a few seconds. This is the way that Jesus was baptised.

▲ At an adult baptism, the person being baptised is lowered into the water backwards. Baptism symbolises the washing away of **sins**.

Confirmation

Many Christians may decide to renew their promises to God when they are older. In the Anglican church this is called Confirmation and it is done during a special service in the church. Confirmation usually takes place when a boy or girl is a teenager, but it can happen at any age.

Christian festivals

Services are held in Christian churches to celebrate different times in the life of Jesus. Christmas is a time to remember his birth. Many Christians go to church for Midnight Mass on Christmas Eve because they believe Jesus was born during the night. There is also a service on the morning of Christmas Day. At this time, the congregation sings **carols** and gives thanks to God for sending His Son to Earth.

▼ Over Christmas many churches put on a nativity play. This shows the birth of Jesus in the stable at Bethlehem. The parts are usually played by children.

Lent

Lent lasts for 40 days. During this time, Christians remember when Jesus went into the desert to think about the work God wanted him to do. At the beginning of Lent, Christians go to church and ask for God's forgiveness for the bad things they have done. People often give up something they enjoy during Lent. This helps them to remember how hard it was for Jesus to be alone in the desert for so long.

Palm Sunday

Palm Sunday is the Sunday before Easter. It is the beginning of **Holy Week**, which leads up to **Good Friday** and the crucifixion of Jesus. On Palm Sunday, Christians remember when Jesus rode into Jerusalem on a donkey. He was welcomed by the people of the city with great joy and happiness. Many of his followers threw palm leaves on the ground for the donkey to walk on.

▲ On Palm Sunday, many Christians around the world take part in processions and carry palm leaves.

Easter

Christians believe that although Jesus was crucified, he rose from the dead three days later. This is called the resurrection and it is celebrated on Easter Sunday by Christians around the world. Easter Sunday is a joyful time. In church, the story of Jesus' death and resurrection is told. Special Easter hymns are sung and prayers are said, thanking God for the life of Jesus.

▶ On Easter Saturday, a special candle called the Paschal candle is lit in some Catholic churches. This is a sign of the coming resurrection of Jesus and the light he will bring into the world.

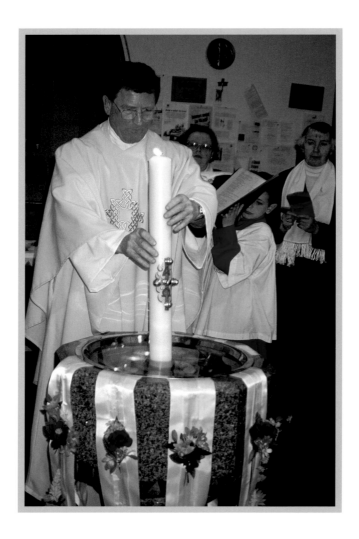

EASTER EGGS

On Easter Sunday, many people give each other chocolate eggs. These are a symbol of life after death and the new life promised to all Christians who believe in Jesus.

▶ Many Christians exchange eggs wrapped in coloured paper to celebrate a bright new beginning.

Pentecost

Christians celebrate Pentecost about 50 days after Easter. Many churches hold special services and people are often baptised on this day. Christians believe that at Pentecost, Jesus' disciples heard a rushing wind and saw tongues of flames. They discovered that they could speak different languages. This meant they were able to spread the word of God.

A good harvest

Harvest Festival is held in the autumn. Many Christians go to special church services to thank God for the harvest and pray for another good harvest in the coming year. People take food to their church just before the festival. It can be fresh or tinned food. After the service, the food is usually given to the elderly and needy in the local community.

▶ During Harvest Festival, a display of fresh fruit, vegetables and flowers is often kept in the church to thank God for His goodness.

Holy places

Many places around the world are important to Christians. A journey to these places is called a pilgrimage and the people who make these journeys are pilgrims. Some special places are Bethlehem where Jesus was born, Nazareth where he grew up, and Jerusalem where he was buried.

▼ Many pilgrims visit the Church of the Holy Sepulchre in Jerusalem. This church is believed to have been built on the place where the body of Jesus was buried after his crucifixion.

Lourdes

Lourdes, in France, is a special place of pilgrimage for Catholics. Every year, thousands of sick people visit Lourdes believing they will be cured if they drink water from the **spring**. It is said a young French girl called Bernadette had a **vision** of the Virgin Mary there. A spring of water appeared where the Virgin Mary stood. Bernadette drank from the spring and was cured of her illness.

▼ A statue of the Virgin Mary is in the cave in Lourdes where Bernadette had her vision.

THE POPE AND ROME

Vatican City in Rome, Italy, is one of the holiest places for Roman Catholics. It is the home of the Pope, who is the head of the Roman Catholic Church.

▲ St Peter's Church in the Vatican is the main church for Catholics.

Glossary

Bible the Christian holy book

carols songs sung at Christmas time that often tell the story of Jesus' birth

choir a group of people who sing in the church and who often lead the singing of hymns

Communion when Christians share bread and wine during a service

Congregation a group of people who go to a church service

crucified when someone is killed by being nailed to a cross

disciples the 12 men who were special followers of Jesus and his teachings

Good Friday the day Jesus was crucified. It was called 'Good Friday' as Christians believe that because Jesus died their sins were forgiven

Heaven Christians believe this is the home of God and a place of great happiness

Holy Week the name for the seven days before Easter

incense spices that are sweet-smelling when they are burning

Jesus a Jewish teacher who began Christianity by teaching the Word of God. Christians believe that Jesus was the Son of God. He is also called Jesus Christ. The word Christ means 'chosen by God'

Jews people who follow the religion of Judaism

Latin an ancient language

miracles amazing and wonderful things that happen that cannot be explained

parables stories that have a special meaning, such as being kind to each other and helping strangers

sins bad actions that break religious laws

spring a small stream of water that comes up from under the ground

stained-glass window a window made of pieces of coloured glass fitted together to make a picture or pattern

vision when a person sees someone who is dead or something that cannot be real

Quizzes

Try these questions to see how much you remember about Christianity.

Are these facts true or false?

1. A chapel is a type of church.

2. The altar is where people are baptised.

3. A crucifix is a cross with Jesus on it.

4. Baptism is a when Christians become part of the church.

5. Easter celebrates the birth of Jesus.

Can you match the name to what you can see in the church?

1. Lectern

2. Font

3. Pews

4. Altar

Answers are on the next page.

Index

Answers:

1 True

2 False, people are baptised at the font

3 True

4 True

5 False, Easter celebrates the death of Jesus and his resurrection

Match the word to the object: 1b, 2d, 3c, 4a

OUR PLACES OF WORSHIP

Contents of titles in the series:

WAYLAND